MORE
Jokes AND Riddles

WHAT IS AN EASY READER?

- This story has been carefully written to capture the interest of the young reader.

- It is told in a simple, direct style with a strong rhythm that adds enjoyment both to reading aloud and silent reading.

- Many key words are repeated regularly throughout the story. This skillful repetition helps the child to read independently. Encountering words again and again, the young reader practices the vocabulary he or she knows, and learns with ease the words that are new.

- Only 270 different words have been used, with plurals and root words counted once.

  More than one-half of the words in this story have been used at least three times.

  Almost one-fourth of the words in this story have been used at least six times.

  Eighteen words have been used at least 10 times.

ABOUT THIS BOOK

- Here are more jokes and riddles to hear or read—then try out on others. This book, a sequel to JOKES AND RIDDLES, is especially recommended as book-bait for the youngster who is still book-shy.

MORe
Jokes AND Riddles

Compiled by JONATHAN PETER
Pictures by ALBERT AQUINO

Editorial Consultant:
LILIAN MOORE

Wonder® Books

PRICE/STERN/SLOAN
Publishers, Inc., Los Angeles
1986

Introduction

Easy Readers help young readers discover what a delightful experience reading can be. The stories are such fun that they inspire children to try new reading skills. They are so easy to read that they provide encouragement and support for children as readers.

The adult will notice that the sentences aren't too long, the words aren't too hard, and the skillful repetition is like a helping hand. What the child will feel is: "This is a good story—and I can read it myself!"

For some children, the best way to meet these stories may be to hear them read aloud at first. Others, who are better prepared to read on their own, may need a little help in the beginning—help that is best given freely. Youngsters who have more experience in reading alone—whether in first or second or third grade—will have the immediate joy of reading "all by myself."

These books have been planned to help all young readers grow—in their pleasure in books and in their power to read them.

Lilian Moore
Specialist in Reading
Formerly of Division of Instructional Research,
New York City Board of Education

"Jane," said Mother,
"how did you get that bump
on your head?"

"Some little beans hit me,"
Jane said.

Mother said, "How could little beans
give you a big bump like that?"

"The beans were in THAT can!"
said Jane.

Why is the policeman the strongest
man in town?

 I give up.

He can hold up many cars
with one hand!

Mother took a good look at Sam.

"Oh, my!"

she said.

"What did you do?"

"I fell in the mud,"

said Sam.

"Oh, Sam!" said Mother.
"With your good pants on?"

"Well," said Sam.
"I did not have time
to take them off."

What has one horn,

runs up and down the street,

and gives milk?

 I give up.

A milk truck!

"Do you see that big horse?"
said Ned.

"Yes," said Ted.
"He is a race horse."

"Well," said Ned.
"I can race him and win."

"Run a race with a race horse?"
said Ted. "Ha! Ha!"

"Yes, I can," said Ned.
"Guess where I can do it."

"Where?" said Ted.

"Up a ladder," said Ned.

Susie ran to her mother, crying.

"What is the matter, Susie?"
her mother asked.

"Look!" said Susie. "Danny put this
in my bed!"

"Danny!" said Mother.

"Why did you do that?

Why did you put a frog

in your sister's bed?"

19

"Well," said Danny,

"I could not find a snake."

Do you know why the corn
does not like the farmer?

 I give up.

The farmer pulls its ears!

Jenny met Penny walking
down the street.
"Why do you have a string
around your finger?" asked Jenny.

"My mother put it on,"
said Penny.

"Why?" asked Jenny.

"She put it on," said Penny,

"so that I would not forget

to mail her letter."

"Did you mail it?" asked Jenny.

"No," said Penny.

"She forgot to give me the letter."

I am so glad I am not a bird.

Guess why?

I give up.

I can't fly!

Billy was playing at Willy's house.

"May I sleep
at your house tonight?"
Billy asked Willy.

"Yes," said Willy.

"You may sleep here.
But you will have to make
your own bed."

"That's all right,"
said Billy.

"You can start now,"

said Willy.

"Here is some wood and a hammer!"

Patty wanted to send a letter.

So she went to buy some stamps.

"May I have two stamps, please?"
she asked the man.

The man gave the stamps to Patty.

Patty looked at them.

"Do I have to stick them on
myself?" she asked.

"No," said the man.

"Just stick them on your letter!"

Everybody in the Hill family
has brown hair — all but Pete.
He has red hair.

One day Jimmy Hill took
his little brother, Pete,
to get a haircut.
The man looked at Jimmy.
Then he looked at Pete.

"Jimmy," he said, "where did
your little brother
get his red hair?"

"I think it grew out of his head,"
said Jimmy.

Why is a hill not like a pill?

 I give up.

A hill is hard to get up

and a pill is hard to get down!

"Guess what!
We have a hen in our barn,"
said Jerry.

"What's so good about that?"
said Terry.

"She lays big white eggs,"
said Jerry.

"What's so good about that?"
said Terry.

"Can YOU lay big white eggs?"
said Jerry.

When can you see cows with 8 feet?

 I give up.

When 2 cows are standing side by side!

Mr. Bungle had to catch a train.
On the way he stopped to eat.

"What will you have?"
asked the waiter.

"I want a glass of milk
and one big pancake, please,"
said Mr. Bungle.

The waiter came back
with the glass of milk.
"I will bring your pancake soon,"
he said.

"I have to catch a train,"
said Mr. Bungle.
"How long will it be?"

"Oh," said the waiter,
"your pancake will not be long
at all. It will be round!"

Tell me two things you can never eat for breakfast.

 I give up.

Lunch and supper!

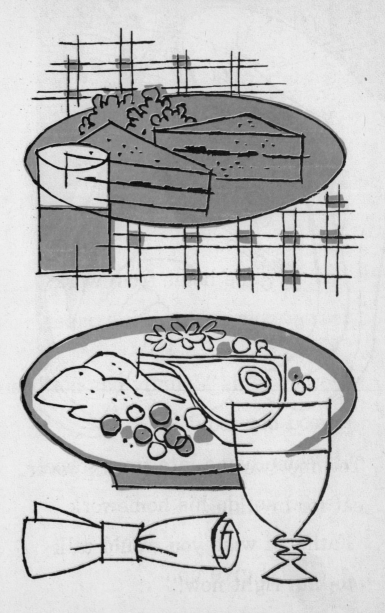

Father came home from work.

He sat down to read his paper.

Mother said, "Johnny has not been
a good boy today.

He came home late from school.

He did not do his homework.

Father, I wish you would talk
to him right now!"

Father looked up from his paper.

"Hello, Johnny," he said.

I saw a brown egg in a green box
on a red table.

Guess where it came from.

I give up.

From a hen!

Jack called to his mother.

"I need help," he said.

But his mother did not come.

"Oh, Jack," she said,

"you always ask for help.

Try to help yourself."

Soon Jack called again.

"I DO need help, Mother.

I DID try.

But I can't push

all this toothpaste back!"

Guess which man has on
the biggest hat.

 I give up.

The man with the biggest head!

One day Mother said to Sally,

"I need some help.

Will you do the sweeping?"

Sally took the broom
and began to sweep.

Soon Mother said,
"Did you sweep the hall, Sally?"

"Yes," said Sally.

"Good!" Mother said.
"Did you sweep behind the door?"

"Oh, yes," said Sally.
"I swept EVERYTHING
behind the door!"

Benny went to the pet store.

He looked at all the birds.

Then he said to the man,

"Please, may I have some bird seed?"

"What kind of bird do you have?"
asked the man.

"Oh," said Benny,

"I do not have a bird.

That's why I want the bird seed.

I want to grow one."

Aquino